EACH PART
WORKING
PROPERLY

MEMBERSHIP AT COMMUNITY FREE CHURCH

EACH PART
WORKING
PROPERLY

MEMBERSHIP AT COMMUNITY FREE CHURCH

SPEAKING THE TRUTH IN LOVE, WE ARE TO GROW UP IN EVERY WAY INTO HIM WHO IS THE HEAD, INTO CHRIST, FROM WHOM THE WHOLE BODY, JOINED AND HELD TOGETHER BY EVERY JOINT WITH WHICH IT IS EQUIPPED, WHEN EACH PART IS WORKING PROPERLY, MAKES THE BODY GROW SO THAT IT BUILDS ITSELF UP IN LOVE.

-EPHESIANS 4:15-16

Community Evangelical Free Church
3640 Ash Street, Harrisburg, Pennsylvania, 17109
www.CommunityFreeChurch.org

Each Part Working Properly was written by Benjamin Vrbicek in collaboration with the other pastor-elders.

Benjamin Vrbicek blogs regularly at <u>BenjaminVrbicek.com</u>.

Cover and interior design: Benjamin Vrbicek
Cover image: depositphotos.com

ISBN (print): 978-1-5170-7704-4

Special thanks to Carolyn Aiken, Jason Abbott, Mary Wells, Alexandra Richter for their editorial assistance and to New Life Bible Fellowship in Tucson, AZ for allowing several sections to be repurposed from previous material.

Version 7.0, October 18, 2020

CONTENTS

INTRODUCTION

Our membership class used to be on a Sunday after church. It was just an hour or two, but it made for a long day.

In the class, a few pastors would share about our church, and we'd do our best to teach the material and answer some questions. Often, however, the whole thing felt rushed. I could tell that someone usually wanted to ask follow-up questions, but at the same time, he didn't want to be "that guy"—you know, the one who keeps people at a meeting that's already too long.

And it wasn't just getting through all of our information that made the class rushed. We, as pastors, also wanted to get to know the people in the class, just as they wanted to get to know us. Yet there wasn't much time for this either.

It was as though we were all at a restaurant to enjoy a good meal with good company, but then we looked at our watches, realized we were out of time, and we had to go. So together, we scarfed down our food and left a little unsatisfied.

Now we have slowed things down. Now the membership class lasts four weeks. During the first three weeks, we cover topics that we think would be helpful to you as you consider what it might mean to join our church. We cover topics such as the meaning of the gospel, our church's history and structure, and our denomination's core theological beliefs.

This may not seem crucial—but trust me, it is.

Let me tell you why with a little story. I have a brother who started attending a church in the Midwest with his family. At first, things seemed great. They liked the pastor, the worship was engaging, and the people were friendly. And so they stayed. But as time went on, they began to have questions about the theology of the church. After a year and a half at the church, my brother told me, "You know, Benjamin, I don't think we would have stayed here if we had known upfront what this church was about." The church wasn't teaching anything heretical. It was just off center a bit, at least from my brother's perspective.

This put them in a place where they had to make a hard decision: *stay*, continuing to invest with people they now considered family or *leave*, following their theological consciences only to start over somewhere else.

We don't want this to happen to you. We care about you. This membership class and this book are expressions of that care. Of course, we believe this is a good church and a good place to worship God; that's why we're here. But you'll need to decide that for yourself, and besides participating in our weekly worship services, the best way for you to make that choice, we believe, is by going through this class.

In addition to your learning about us, we hope to learn about you throughout the class as well. That's especially what the last week is about. During Week 4, there is no "material" per se; we dedicate all of the time in class for you to take turns sharing some of what God has done in your life. This will take place among the people that you've sat at the same tables with throughout the class. For some, perhaps even you, this sharing about what God has done in your life sounds like a scary thing. But it shouldn't be, and we'll do our best to prepare you for it.

Finally, in this class we hope that you'll find a ministry, or several ministries, for you to serve in. We want you to find a place to use the gifts that God has given you. Growing churches can be misleading. Newcomers see all of the activity and think, "There's no place here for me to serve."

Wrong.

We may have a lot going on, but we want you—in fact, we *need* you—just as a healthy family needs all of its members. It's through the power of the gospel, "when each part is working properly" (Ephesians 4:15), that God builds his church in love.

And you were dead in the trespasses and sins.... But God ...

- Paul, chief of sinners

FIRST THINGS FIRST

In the Introduction, when discussing the importance of knowing what a church believes before you join, I mentioned my brother and his family. I mentioned how they wished they had known up-front what their church believed before they committed. In Week 2, we'll get into the specifics of our denomination's theology, but at this point, let's dive into what our church believes about two topics, namely, the gospel and local church membership.

WHAT IS THE GOSPEL?

Christians use the word "gospel" all the time. We talk of gospel services, gospel preaching, gospel truth, and gospel songs. We can talk of The Gospels as specific books in the Bible, and we can also speak of the gospel-story, that is, the overarching story that permeates the whole Bible.

So what *do* we mean when we talk of this thing called "the gospel"?

Well, speaking very broadly, the word gospel means "good news." The gospel is *news*—news that is *good*.

But here's where it gets tricky. Here's where we need to be more precise. What specifically is the content of this news? And what, specifically, is it that makes this news good?

There are lots of ways to say it

If you asked one hundred Christians these questions, I'm not sure that you'd get one hundred different responses, but you'd get several dozen. Some of the responses would be good and others would not.

The variation in the replies—at least of the good responses—is not necessarily a bad thing. At Community, we readily acknowledge that there are many helpful ways to communicate the content of the gospel; there isn't just one correct way to say it. It's possible to use different overarching metaphors and emphasize different biblical passages. Some will be familiar with presentations of the gospel such as "The Roman Road," which, as you would expect, emphasizes a series of passages from Romans. Others will know of Campus Crusade's "Four Spiritual Laws," or Evangelism Explosion's series of questions, or "The Way of the Master" from Ray Comfort, and on and on it goes.

It's not only modern presentations of the gospel that vary; variation occurs inside the Bible itself. For example, Luke can explain the gospel a little different than John and Peter a little different than Paul. At times, there is even variation within the writings from the same author. Paul, for example, emphasizes different motifs and metaphors to describe the gospel. He emphasizes "reconciliation" in 2 Corinthians 5, "near and far" in Ephesians 2, and "humiliation and exaltation" in Philippians 2.

On top of all this variation, there is added variation in length. For example, sometimes the gospel can be described by Paul in just a few verses, as in 1 Corinthians 15:1–6, but in another sense, we might consider the entire letter of Romans a gospel presentation.

All of this variation, however, does not mean that there are not core elements of the gospel that each author affirms—or would affirm. There *are* core elements of the gospel, even if individual authors (biblical authors or post-biblical authors) explain these fundamentals in different ways, with different words, different metaphors, and different lengths. And it's these core elements of the good news that we want to talk about now.

If you distilled the gospel to its core, we believe you could do so under these two headings: *The victory of Jesus* and *justification by faith alone*.

Allow me to unpack what we mean by each.

First, it's the good news of the victory of Jesus

In the beginning God created a good world, indeed it was "very good" (Genesis 1:31). There was peace and harmony among all of creation. All was right with Adam and Eve. This was true as they related to each other and as they related to their God. It truly was paradise. God walked with his people in the "cool of the day" (Genesis 3:8). There was *shalom*; things were the way they were supposed to be.

But things did not stay this way.

Sin and death were introduced when Adam and Eve chose to rebel against God. God gave them very specific instructions, but they did not obey. Our first parents attempted to find happiness and significance apart from God. They listened to the lie of the serpent.

Consequently, what was pure and pristine became polluted. Paradise was lost not only for Adam and Eve but for all subsequent generations. When they disobeyed God, Adam plunged future generations into sin and death (Romans 5:12). Creation was cursed, death was introduced as punishment, and fellowship with God was broken.

Yet, even in the story of death in Genesis 3, we see the promise of hope, the promise of victory, and the promise that one day someone would be born who would forever crush evil and the Evil One. In short, a rescuer would come.

In Genesis 3:15, as God is administering to Satan his curse, we read,

> I will put enmity between you and the woman,
>   and between your offspring and her offspring;
> he shall bruise your head,
>   and you shall bruise his heel.

Although short, these few words are tremendously significant. In them, God promises that one day there will be an offspring of a woman, and that offspring will "crush the head" of the serpent. That's why this verse is often referred to as the *protoevangelium*, the first gospel (*proto* means first and *evangelium* means gospel).

But this is not all we learn from the promise. We also learn that this victory will be a costly victory, as seen when God states, "you shall bruise his heel." This means that Satan "shall bruise [the] heel [of the woman's offspring]."

As the Old Testament presses forward, anticipation of the coming "serpent crusher" grows. Perhaps the image of a snowball rolling down a hill is appropriate; with each new chapter in the biblical story, details of the expectation about the coming Messiah grow larger and larger.

For example, later we learn that the Messiah will not just be any offspring of a woman, but that he will be from the particular family line of King David, and unlike previous heirs to the throne, this King will rule on the throne forever (2 Samuel 7:16).

In other places, we learn that the Savior will be marked by purity and integrity (Isaiah 53:9).

Elsewhere we learn of the Messiah's power (Isaiah 9:6, 7).

Still in other places we learn that the Messiah's mission will involve a great ingathering of Gentiles into the people of God (Isaiah 49:6).

And so the snowball grows in size and speed.

If we were to go back in time to ask an Old Testament believer what he or she anticipated, perhaps we might hear them answer something like this:

> One day a Savior will come …
> he will administer a costly defeat of sin and evil …
> he will ascend to the everlasting throne of his
>   father David …
> he will be known by his faithfulness and power …
> and he will inaugurate a great ingathering of people into
>   an everlasting kingdom characterized by steadfast
>   love, justice, and righteousness.

This is the great hope of Old Testament believers—a powerful Serpent-Crusher, a Davidic-King, and a Suffering-Messiah.

And when we come to the New Testament, we see the biblical authors functioning like journalists whose passion is publishing the good news that Jesus Christ is the one who gloriously fulfills these Old Testament expectations.

These authors say Jesus is the one who crushes the head of the serpent (1 Corinthians 15:24; Colossians 2:15; Hebrews 2:14). Jesus is the one who lives a sinless life (Hebrews 4:15; 1 Peter 2:22; 1 John 3:5). Jesus is the one who suffers greatly—that is, has his heel bruised—through his sacrificial death on the cross (Mark 10:32–34, 45). But Jesus is also the one who rises from the dead, and when he does, Jesus ascends to the throne of King David (Romans 1:1–6; 2 Timothy 2:8). From there, Jesus inaugurates the time when a vast number of people, especially Gentile-outsiders, are drawn into the kingdom (Matthew 12:14–21).

This—the victory of King Jesus—is newsworthy material. It is good news. It's *the* gospel. Jesus has won; the war is over; the King reigns.

However, one thing that was not as clear in the Old Testament, but becomes clear in the New, is that the victory of Jesus is to be achieved in two stages, namely by a *first* and a *second* coming to earth.

Today, we live in the in-between time, the time between Jesus's comings. This is a time when sin and death have been defeated, but their full effects have not been completely put away. It's a time when Jesus sits on a throne at his father's side, but the universal recognition of his reign still awaits (Philippians 2:9–11).

One day, Jesus will come again for everyone to acknowledge him as Lord (Philippians 2:10). What a glorious day that will be for believers—a day when what was lost in the fall of Adam and Eve will be fully restored. A day when

> the dwelling place of God is with man … [and] He will wipe away every tear from [his people's] eyes, and death shall be no more, neither shall there be mourning, nor crying, nor pain anymore … [and Jesus says] "It is done!" (Revelation 21:3–4, 6)

The announcement of the good news of the victory of Jesus is the first thing we mean when we talk about the gospel.

Second, it's the good news of justification by faith alone

While the news of the victory of Jesus is very, very good news, questions still remain. How do individual people obtain the blessings that flow from Jesus's victory? And how do I, as a child of Adam and Eve—with my wicked, sinful nature—actually receive any benefit from the victory of Jesus? Do not I, a guilty sinner, deserve to be defeated during the conquest of the victory of Jesus?

To answer these questions we turn to the second of our headings under which the gospel finds meaning, namely, *justification by faith alone*.

This phrase—justification by faith alone—may feel like a mouthful, as justification is not a word we use in everyday life. It is, however, an important word, one often used in the Bible, and thus a word worth explaining. One popular theology textbook defines justification in this way:

> Justification is an instantaneous legal act of God in which he (1) thinks of our sins as forgiven and Christ's righteousness as belonging to us, and (2) declares us to be righteous in his sight. (Wayne Grudem, *Systematic Theology*, 723)

That may also feel like a mouthful.

Perhaps a shorter way to define it would be to say this: Justification means to be made or considered right, and in the context of the Bible and Christian theology, justification means to be made right in the sight of God.

When we say this, two things are implied. First, God does not count our sins against us, and second, God views us as though we have the perfect obedience that Jesus has (i.e., the righteousness of Christ).

Still feel like a mouthful? Let's look at one passage where this exchange—*our sins are removed and put on Christ,* and *his righteousness is given to us*—is clearly stated. The passage is 2 Corinthians 5:21. For the sake of clarity, I have removed a few of the pronouns (he, him, we) and inserted the name to whom each pronoun is referring (either God, Jesus, or Christians). The verse reads,

God made Jesus to be sin (who knew no sin), so that in Jesus, Christians might become the righteousness of God.

There are two parts to the verse. First, it says, "God made Jesus to be sin." This is a radical statement. Ponder it slowly, one word at a time:

God. Made. Jesus. To. Be. Sin.

What could this possibly mean? How could Jesus be made "to be sin"?

The answer that the Bible puts forward is that Jesus was made to be sin on the cross when all of the sins of God's people were credited to Jesus as though he had done the actual sins himself. This means that on the cross, it could be said that Jesus became the vilest and wicked sinner who ever lived!

But this is only one part of the exchange that takes place in justification. The other part of the exchange is when God gives Christians the righteousness of Christ. That is to say, Christians are viewed as though they lived the perfect life that Jesus actually lived. This is exactly the point made in the second part of verse 21: "so that in Jesus, Christians might become the righteousness of God."

Again, this is incredible and worth pondering one word at a time.

So that ... Christians. Might. Become. The. Righteousness. Of. God.

Indeed this is good news for those who become Christians. The only question that remains is: How? How do I obtain access to this exchange, an exchange where I trade my sins for perfection? Do I need to work really hard? Do I need to be a really moral person?

The answer the Bible gives—and it is good news!—is that through faith in Jesus, apart from our good works, God justifies us. Perhaps one of the clearest passages that describes the "by faith alone" aspect of "justification by faith alone" is in Ephesians 2:1–10. It teaches that though we were once sinners, through Jesus Christ, apart from works, God freely saves those who trust in him.

> And you were dead in the trespasses and sins in which you once walked … we all once lived in the passions of our flesh, carrying out the desires of the body and the mind, and were by nature children of wrath…. But God, being rich in mercy, because of the great love with which He loved us … made us alive together with Christ … *For by grace you have been saved through faith. And this is not your own doing; it is the gift of God, not a result of works, so that no one may boast.*

A person does not come to know God simply because they are *smarter* than others. If that were so, he or she could boast. Nor does a person come to know God because they *try harder* than others. If that were so, he or she could boast. Nor does a person come to know God because they are *more holy* than others. If that were so, he or she could boast.

Rather, as the passage says, "For by grace you have been saved through faith. And this is not your own doing; it is the gift of God." We do not add to God's salvation, nor do we do anything to deserve it. It is a gift received simply by trusting in Jesus—or we might say, simply by faith alone.

For all these reasons, the gospel is paramount at Community. We believe it is the foundation of everything we do at our church. (We'll say more about that next week.) And we wholeheartedly affirm with the Apostle Paul that the gospel is a matter of "first importance" (1 Corinthians 15:3).

We hope and pray that everyone who spends time with our church—in either small or large ways—will see and savor this good news. And we hope and pray that this good news will become the very heartbeat of our church as we spend lifetimes—and eternities—enjoying the riches of the gospel.

IS LOCAL CHURCH MEMBERSHIP EVEN BIBLICAL?

Before ending this chapter, there's one more topic we need to cover. It might feel like a step backward, but it's not. It's more of a step forward. When a person believes the gospel, they become part of God's family, the church (John 1:12). Thus, it makes sense to follow a discussion of the gospel with a conversation about what the gospel produces.

One of the questions I am frequently asked has to do with the big-picture validity of local church membership. People want to know—and I think rightly—that local church membership, as it is practiced in the modern, Western world is actually biblical.

On the one hand, there are some who say that local church membership is entirely a human invention, a product of Western culture and absent from the Bible itself. Their arguments tend to be based more upon what they do not see in the Bible rather than what they do see. In other words, to them there appears to be a lack of evidence in the Bible for membership rather than evidence explicitly against such a thing. An older, wiser Christian man that I deeply respect—a man who has been a long-time leader and elder in several local churches—tends toward this view.

On the other hand, some find strong biblical precedent for local church membership. This, they argue, is seen especially in the book of Acts where it seems that the early church kept track of new "members" (cf. the variations of the repeated phrase "and many were added to their number" in Acts 2:41, 47; 5:14;

11:24; or similarly 16:5). Additionally, in 1 Timothy 5:11–16 it appears that something like a list of specific widows exists. Perhaps this hints at something like local church membership.

Those in favor of membership point out that the New Testament letters to local churches in specific cities may lend credence to the notion of church membership. For example, if you read chapter 16 in Romans, it seems that Paul is not writing to random believers in Rome who are unknown to him or the local church leaders there, but rather Paul knows fully which believers are involved in that church. This is particularly cogent given that at the time Paul wrote the letter, he had not yet been to the church himself (Romans 1:11–13; 15:22–29). Of course, someone might push back on this point by noting that just because some within a church had knowledge of who was part of their church, it does not mean there was a formal membership process. Indeed, this could be true.

But another point to consider is that in the early church—as in every age—there were those who embraced the true gospel and those who did not. All too often, orthodoxy and heterodoxy abided in the same city (cf. 2 Corinthians 11:4; 2 John 7–11). In short, there were good local churches and bad local churches. Thus it was imperative for individual Christians to make a conscious choice regarding which bunch of Christians they would and would not identify with. Might we call this conscious choice a form of membership? Perhaps.

There are other points worthy of consideration that we will save for another day, but I will mention a few matters in passing. First, how modern (or Western) really is church membership and does it not actually have roots deep in church history? Second, how did the presence of persecution in the early church influence the need for formal membership? For example, was there really a need for the *First Baptist Church of Rome* to have a formal membership process under the reign of Nero? I doubt it. The stakes were so high it was unnecessary. Third, do the New Testament commands that leaders "shepherd the flock of God that is among [them]" (1 Peter 5:2; Hebrews 13:17) presume a list of members? A farmer knows *his* sheep from *his neighbor's* sheep, right? Finally, can we infer the reality of membership from the mention of "insiders" and the practice of excommunication in 1 Corinthians 5 (cf. Galatians 6:10; Colossians 4:5) or the mention of a "majority" in 2 Corinthians 6:2?

As I try to weigh all of the points above, my own take on membership lands somewhere between the two views—somewhere between a clear biblical precedent for modern church membership on the one hand and something manufactured to inculcate biblical realities on the other.

Thus, if someone was adamant with me that modern church membership is fabricated, I could see myself responding like this:

> Okay, you may be right. Maybe local church membership, especially in its formal nature, is not in the Bible. And because I believe that people should obey their conscience, if you don't ever join a church, that is fine with me.

> However, even if you do not become a formal member of any church, the Bible encourages you, as a Christian, to pick only one local church at any given time and to make that one particular local church your church "home," even if your commitment is never formally stated.

If in our conversation about whether membership is biblical or not, we were able to separate the formal membership *process*—let's call this "the vehicle"—from the *realities* that are behind church membership—let's call this "the destination"—then the hesitancies I expressed above become much less qualified. I am strongly in favor of the reality that local church membership engenders ("the destination"), for it is clearly biblical. It is simply the formal nature of the process ("the vehicle") that seems manufactured. The only real question for me is *how* do we get there—that is, to the realities behind biblical membership—not *should* we get there.

You see, what we want to strongly discourage is people continually hopping from church to church or going to multiple churches at the same time. When people do this, they often do it under the guise of being "really ministered to." And although this is commonplace in America—perhaps rampant is a better word—lack of commitment to particular people and a particular church cannot be found in the Bible. In fact, just the opposite is found.

The reality is that people who frequently move from church to church tend to become consumers of religious goods and services, not co-laborers in the gospel. And the same could be said of those who go to a Wednesday night Bible study at one church, a Saturday night service at another church, and a Sunday morning service elsewhere. These people tend to become spiritually unhealthy rather than healthy.

The path to true maturity involves commitment to particular people through good times and bad, not religious consumerism. Once people embrace the gospel by faith and become reconciled to God, then they become disciples. And discipleship, among other things, is an intentional rolling-up of your sleeves among particular people. Discipleship is the renouncing of halfhearted commitment to any one church or having each foot in a different church.

I would also add that in light of the transient nature of our culture, the creation of a formal agreement to submit to the leadership and guidance of a particular church—which is a part of the membership agreement—is very prudent and helpful. I do not say this because church leaders, such as me, need willing subjects to boss around. We are not.

Formally declaring a humble posture of learning and service toward particular brothers and sisters tends to create a biblical environment where people work through differences, rather than a place where disagreeing people take their ball and go home. So often, it is only on the backside of hurts and difficulties that real Christian fellowship—the sturdy, gospel kind of fellowship our God desires—can take place. The present state of affairs in the American church of easily offended, noncommittal church-goers is far from the ideal picture described by Paul in Ephesians 4:15–16, where

> speaking the truth in love, we are to grow up in every way into him who is the head, into Christ, from whom the whole body, joined and held together by every joint with which it is equipped, when each part is working properly, makes the body grow so that it builds itself up in love.

Consider also the several dozen "one to another" commands in Scripture (e.g., love one another, serve one another, forgive one another, care for one another, be kind to one another, sing to one another, etc.). These commands become nearly unintelligible without the creation and maintenance of deep relationships within the body of Christ, the type of bonds formally created in membership.

Now, let me address an objection. Some might say, Yes, this is true, but could not all of this "identifying" with one particular local church be done informally? Perhaps people could informally show which church they belong to by combining actions such as regular church attendance, financial giving, involvement in ministries, and investment in relationships.

To me, this is sort of like "common law church membership." It's better to make the reality formal and avoid the ambiguity. It helps everyone. And the modern process of church membership seems like as good a way as any to reinforce this identification, an identification that is itself thoroughly biblical.

So in summary, I do think it is helpful for Christians to formally declare one particular local church—and the people of it—with which they are going to identify. But at the end of the day, having a formal church membership process is a decision for individual Christians and local churches.

As for the pastor-elders at Community, we think it's the right thing. But regardless of where you come down on this issue, what is surely not up for discussion is this: commitment. Christians must make a real commitment to a particular church and its people.

OUR PROCESS TO JOIN

Speaking of making the membership commitment formal, you may be wondering how one does that at our church. It's certainly not a complicated process, but there are a few steps, and it can take a month or two. But by participating in this class and reading this book, you are taking the first step.

At the end of the class, you'll turn in a short membership application. That's the mechanism that lets us know you are interested in going further.

After you turn in the application, we'll be in touch with you to set up a meeting with a few of our pastor-elders. We typically have the meetings after church on Sundays, but we can find other times if that doesn't work for your schedule. In that meeting, we'll talk about how you became a Christian and about what ministries you might be interested in joining. Also, there will be plenty of time to answer any leftover questions you might have for us.

After this meeting, the pastor-elders will then debrief with each other at our next elder meeting. Honestly, there are rarely any issues, but sometimes after we get to know a person better, we realize there might be something worth talking about with them in more detail. For example, maybe there are issues at a previous church that a person needs to work through before they join us. Or sometimes it appears that a person is not actually a Christian yet. This would be something that we'd want to follow up with. I don't mention this to scare you. In fact, we hope it would encourage you that we take our role as pastor-elders seriously and that we want to see God's church grow in a healthy way.

The final step is to put your name in the church bulletin for two weeks, and then on the third week, we will take time during the worship service to formally welcome you and pray for you.

If any of that didn't make sense, please be sure to ask. We'll probably say it several times throughout the class.

Next week, we'll begin to talk more about our church history and what our denomination believes. We encourage you to read ahead and come with questions.

Contend for the faith that was once for all delivered to the saints.

- Jude, a half-brother of Jesus

FROM POST-IT NOTES TO STATEMENTS OF FAITH

I used to be an engineer in the construction industry. It was a good job—demanding, but good. I even had my own cubicle, which was pretty nice, at least as far as cubicles go.

One day my boss, who also happened to be the son of the president of our company, came up behind me and slapped a *Post-it* note down on my desk. It made a loud thud.

In a friendly but determined voice, he said, "That's it. We're going to get to the bottom of this. On a *Post-it* note, you are going to write what you believe faith in God is all about. And I'm going to do the same thing. Then we are going to discuss and finally get to the bottom of this."

I was taken aback. But I can say that his words didn't come out of nowhere. My boss (we'll call him Steven) and I had been having some good dialogue over the last few years about faith. You see, Steven was very religious and even believed in Jesus, but from my perspective, his Jesus was a very different Jesus than the one presented in the Bible. Generally, our conversations were respectful and even cordial, but we often struggled to put our differences into words.

Throughout church history, disputes like this have been common. When the dispute was large enough, sometimes leaders would convene a church council to decide the matter. At other times, people wrote thick books back and forth. But Steven and I, we turned to the trusty *Post-it* note to sort it out.

At first, I thought the task of articulating the core of what Christians believe would be easy. After all, I had been around Christianity all my life. And when Steven and I did this I was enrolled in seminary full-time.

But it wasn't easy.

It took time.

It took thought.

It took research.

Yet it was necessary, both for my conversation with Steven and for my growth as a Christian.

How would you respond if you were in my place? What things do you believe are at the core of Christianity? Or to put it another way (and shift the focus slightly), what are the chief doctrines that all Christians should believe?

Perhaps these are things you have never taken time to think about, at least formally. So maybe we should do that now. On a piece of scrap paper or a *Post-it* note (or below in the space provided), take a few minutes to jot down the answer to this question:

What are the most important aspects of Christianity?

1. _____

2. _____

3. _____

4. _____

5. _____

Obviously, a *Post-it* note doesn't allow for much space to write, and it's a long ways away from convening a church council, but you get the idea.

When I filled out my *Post-it* note for Steven, I jotted down the following seven points:

1. God
2. Bible
3. Man
4. Salvation
5. Christian Living
6. The Church
7. Eternity

There was no magic in the number seven, but at the time, it seemed to be a good way to organize my thoughts. As the weeks went on, Steven and I eventually abandoned the *Post-it* note and moved to a typed sheet of paper so that we could better elaborate our beliefs. I remember this time well because it was over a semester break, which means I gave way more time to it than I probably should have, but again, it was a helpful process for both of us, I think.

The Evangelical Free Church of America (EFCA), which is the denomination that Community is part of, has done a similar thing. No, they didn't use a *Post-it* note, and no, they didn't use seven points. But they did use ten.

Please take the time to read these ten points listed below. They come from a document called "The Evangelical Free Church of America Statement of Faith." In class, we will go over this in more detail, but it will be helpful to our conversation if you have looked at it beforehand and thought of questions. We think it's a great resource to understand what Community believes is at the core of Christianity. Also, if you are interested, you can find an expanded version of the statement of faith online that includes all of the Scripture references, which are extensive.

THE EFCA STATEMENT OF FAITH

The Evangelical Free Church of America is an association of autonomous churches united around these theological convictions:

God

> 1. We believe in one God, Creator of all things, holy, infinitely perfect, and eternally existing in a loving unity of three equally divine Persons: the Father, the Son and the Holy Spirit. Having limitless knowledge and sovereign power, God has graciously purposed from eternity to redeem a people for Himself and to make all things new for His own glory.

The Bible

> 2. We believe that God has spoken in the Scriptures, both Old and New Testaments, through the words of human authors. As the verbally inspired Word of God, the Bible is without error in the original writings, the complete revelation of His will for salvation, and the ultimate authority by which every realm of human knowledge and endeavor should be judged. Therefore, it is to be believed in all that it teaches, obeyed in all that it requires, and trusted in all that it promises.

The Human Condition

> 3. We believe that God created Adam and Eve in His image, but they sinned when tempted by Satan. In union with Adam, human beings are sinners by nature and by choice, alienated from God, and under His wrath. Only

through God's saving work in Jesus Christ can we be rescued, reconciled and renewed.

Jesus Christ

4. We believe that Jesus Christ is God incarnate, fully God and fully man, one Person in two natures. Jesus—Israel's promised Messiah—was conceived through the Holy Spirit and born of the virgin Mary. He lived a sinless life, was crucified under Pontius Pilate, arose bodily from the dead, ascended into heaven and sits at the right hand of God the Father as our High Priest and Advocate.

The Work of Christ

5. We believe that Jesus Christ, as our representative and substitute, shed His blood on the cross as the perfect, all-sufficient sacrifice for our sins. His atoning death and victorious resurrection constitute the only ground for salvation.

The Holy Spirit

6. We believe that the Holy Spirit, in all that He does, glorifies the Lord Jesus Christ. He convicts the world of its guilt. He regenerates sinners, and in Him they are baptized into union with Christ and adopted as heirs in the family of God. He also indwells, illuminates, guides, equips and empowers believers for Christ-like living and service.

The Church

7. We believe that the true church comprises all who have been justified by God's grace through faith alone in Christ alone. They are united by the Holy Spirit in the body of

Christ, of which He is the Head. The true church is manifest in local churches, whose membership should be composed only of believers. The Lord Jesus mandated two ordinances, baptism and the Lord's Supper, which visibly and tangibly express the gospel. Though they are not the means of salvation, when celebrated by the church in genuine faith, these ordinances confirm and nourish the believer.

Christian Living

8. We believe that God's justifying grace must not be separated from His sanctifying power and purpose. God commands us to love Him supremely and others sacrificially, and to live out our faith with care for one another, compassion toward the poor and justice for the oppressed. With God's Word, the Spirit's power, and fervent prayer in Christ's name, we are to combat the spiritual forces of evil. In obedience to Christ's commission, we are to make disciples among all people, always bearing witness to the gospel in word and deed.

Christ's Return

9. We believe in the personal, bodily and glorious return of our Lord Jesus Christ. The coming of Christ, at a time known only to God, demands constant expectancy and, as our blessed hope, motivates the believer to godly living, sacrificial service and energetic mission.

Response and Eternal Destiny

10. We believe that God commands everyone everywhere to believe the gospel by turning to Him in repentance and receiving the Lord Jesus Christ. We believe that God will

raise the dead bodily and judge the world, assigning the unbeliever to condemnation and eternal conscious punishment and the believer to eternal blessedness and joy with the Lord in the new heaven and the new earth, to the praise of His glorious grace. Amen.

THE SIGNIFICANCE OF SILENCE

There is a lot of rich doctrine crammed into that statement of faith. That's what we love about it. We love that in just a little over 700 words, the most central aspects of the faith are stated with clarity and biblical fidelity.

But as rich as the statement of faith is, and as full of gospel-doctrine as it is, it's still missing some things. There are still many issues not covered. Actually, this is intentional. It's what many in the EFCA call "the significance of silence." This means that there are some things, even important things, that as a denomination we leave for individual churches to decide.

All of this "silence," of course, is done within the bounds of orthodoxy. Thus, we're not talking about silence over things explicitly affirmed in the statement of faith, things such as the triune nature of God, the inerrancy of Scripture, the full divinity and humanity of Jesus, the necessity for sinful humans to receive forgiveness from God through the person and work of Jesus, the second coming of Jesus, and the binary state of eternal destiny in either the new heavens and new earth or hell. Statements like these are nonnegotiable. They are essentials. In them, we must have unity.

Here is how it is explained in *Evangelical Convictions,* published by the EFCA, pp. 24–25 (emphasis original):

> Once [the early Free Church leaders] began to put in writing what was commonly believed among them, they were *silent* on those doctrines which through the centuries had

divided Christians of *equal dedication, Biblical knowledge, spiritual maturity and love for Christ*. This "significance of silence" reflected our strong concern for Evangelical unity in the gospel.

So if we are not talking primarily about issues of orthodoxy, what then do we have in mind? What issues are we "silent" on as a denomination? I won't take the time to list them all, but I will mention a few of them. The EFCA has no agreed-upon position on the continuation or the cessation of the sign gifts (speaking in tongues, prophecy, healing); the age of the earth (young or old); meaning and mode of baptism; and the relationship between God's sovereignty and human responsibility.

Perhaps the name "silence" could be misleading. Are we saying that to be silent means we shouldn't ever talk about these issues or must be ambivalent toward them or settle for a "theology of the lowest common denominator"?

No, not at all.

It's good and right for every local church and pastor-elder team to promote healthy discussion on these issues so that, together, we might develop clear, biblical convictions about them. Community does this; our pastor-elders do this. We frequently discuss theology and hold classes on specific topics. And as an elder board, we are often reading books together to grow in our understanding.

At this point, let's talk about some of the specific views that tend to be held among the pastor-elders at Community.

THE THEOLOGICAL DNA OF OUR PASTOR-ELDERS

There's no point here in trying to be exhaustive. Here is what we'll discuss next: (1) Gospel-Centeredness, (2) Believer's Baptism, (3) the Historic Premillennial & Amillennial Return of Jesus, (4) Reformed Theology, and (5) Complementarianism.

Each is worthy of a five-week Sunday school class, not a five-sentence mention-in-passing. But I'll do my best. If you want to pursue these more, please do so. We'll be happy to talk about them in class or over coffee—especially if you are buying.

I'll start with, shall we say, the least controversial and move to the most controversial.

(1) Gospel-Centeredness

What is gospel-centeredness? It's this: we desperately want to see the gospel of Jesus Christ wash all of life—that is, we center everything on the gospel.

We talked extensively about the gospel in Week 1, but in short, the gospel is the good news that Jesus Christ lived the life we should have lived, died the death we should have died and rose again defeating death forever (1 Corinthians 15:3–4). By grace alone, through faith alone, in Christ alone, his perfect life is transferred to our account, and our record of sin was taken by Christ to the cross where he received the wrath of God and rejection we deserved (2 Corinthians 5:21). Astonishment over this should be the heartbeat of every ministry of the church—informing and shaping the way we go about even the smallest details of ministry (1 Corinthians 15:1–2).

Therefore, gospel-centeredness bleeds into our passion for the Word of God as not merely an intellectual pursuit, but a pursuit born out of astonishment at the grace of God in giving us his very words in a book.

Gospel-centeredness bleeds into our desire for authentic community, the kind marked by deep and caring relationships. It is the gospel that enables us to embody a culture of repentance, forgiveness, growth in Christlikeness, prayer, and joy (Acts 2:46–47).

Gospel-centeredness means that we live on mission, the mission to see disciples multiplied throughout Harrisburg and the world.

And gospel-centeredness propels us into sacrificial service, the kind that loves others in our city, regardless of whether they follow Jesus or not. Christ's love for outsiders, like us (Romans 5:8), propels our church toward acts of service, care for the poor, and a willingness to lay our lives down for our neighbors.

This is what we mean by gospel-centeredness.

(2) Believer's Baptism

The next distinctive to discuss is baptism. It's an important issue. Jesus commanded that it be done (Matthew 28:19–20), and it was clearly a significant part of the early church, as evidenced by the number of times it was practiced in the book of Acts (2:38, 41; 8:12, 36; 10:48; and so on) and mentioned in the Epistles (Romans 6:3–4; 1 Corinthians 1:13–17; Galatians 3:27; Ephesians 4:5; Colossians 2:11–12; and 1 Peter 3:21).

At our church, we practice believer's baptism, which is sometimes called *credo*-baptism (*credo* means belief). This view is over and against infant baptism, also called covenantal-baptism or *paedo*-baptism (*paedo* means of a child).

Those who hold to believer's baptism, as we do, understand that once a person has experienced the saving power of the gospel, it is appropriate to display what has happened on the inside with a sign on the outside. In this way, baptism is much like wearing a wedding ring—it displays to the world that the person is in an exclusive relationship with another. The ring—and baptism—do not put a person in this relationship; they symbolize it.

Those who believe in infant baptism, on the other hand, believe that baptism in the New Testament functions much like the sign of circumcision in the Old Testament. That is to say, covenantal-baptism is the view that baptism is a sign appropriate for all those associated with the covenant people of God (infant or not). In this view, if the person baptized is an infant, then that infant must one day make the personal decision to embrace the faith from the heart (just as those who were circumcised as infants had to do). This is what infant baptism means, at least in the Presbyterian view. Lutherans and Catholics, however, mean something more specific, and frankly, something unhelpful and untrue. Lutherans and Catholics believe that, in infant baptism, original sin (in some way, shape, or form) is washed away. This is certainly not taught in the Bible. Thus, while there are some EFCA churches that practice infant baptism (and I was a member of one several years ago), they would only do so within the Presbyterian framework.

Before moving on, perhaps I should add just one more thing. We do not require baptism for membership, though we certainly encourage it if you have not been baptized. Thus, it's something we will typically discuss with you in your meeting with the pastor-elders if you pursue the next step of membership (see Week 1, "Our Process to Join").

(3) The Historic Premillennial & Amillennial Return of Jesus

Views on the end times have always been tricky in Christianity. Today, some Christians have charts that plot out what they believe to be the specifics of Jesus's return. Others, perhaps put-off by the charts, tend to fall into the "pan-millennial" view. The pan-millennial view is the view that "it will all pan-out in the end." (Sorry, this is a silly pastor joke. Please forgive me for perpetuating it.)

The EFCA statement of faith formerly specified a "premillennial return of Jesus" (Article 9, Christ's Return, "We believe in the personal, bodily and _premillennial_ return of our Lord Jesus Christ"). Therefore, churches in the EFCA used to only take one of two views on the tribulation and millennium: either historic premillennialism or dispensationalism. However, in the summer of 2019 the statement of faith was broadened to include all orthodox views of the return of Christ, including amillennial and postmillennial views (Article 9, Christ's Return, now reads, "We believe in the personal, bodily and _glorious_ return of our Lord Jesus Christ"). This is not the place to teach extensively on the differing views, but perhaps I should explain them briefly.

With respect to the tribulation, many Christians interpret this term to refer to a period of intense struggle, calamity, and persecution, or as Jesus says, a "great tribulation" (Matthew 24:21). Two central questions in this conversation are: when will this "great tribulation" happen, and will the church experience it or be raptured from it?

Our pastor-elders tend to ascribe to one of two views, namely, historic premillennialism or amillennialism. **Historic premillennialism** understands the Bible to teach that the church as a whole will remain throughout this tribulation period, and after a time, Jesus will return to set up his millennial kingdom on earth. Historic premillennialism understands the Bible, particularly Revelation 20:1–6, to teach that there will be a 1,000-year time (a millennium) in which Satan is bound and believers are resurrected to live with Christ while he reigns on earth. Later, Satan will be released, and there will be a final rebellion. After this comes the resurrection of all people, the final judgment, and the establishment of the eternal state, that is, the new heavens and the new earth.

Amillennialism rightly understood does not deny the existence of the millennium as atheism denies the existence of God; rather, amillennialism understands the Bible to speak of Christ's millennial reign to be taking place in heaven right now. The amillennial view is consistent with passages that intricately link the timing of Christ's return with the final judgment and eternal state (Romans 8:17–23; 2 Thessalonians 1:5–10; 2 Peter 3:3–14).

The other premillennial view is **dispensationalism**. This view sees two future returns of Christ: first, a "secret" or pre-tribulation return of Christ to rapture his church from the world before the tribulation and then yet another return to set up his millennial kingdom. Although it's not the best representation of this view, the popular *Left Behind* series is based on a dispensational understanding of the end times.

Postmillennialism teaches that Jesus will return after a time of blessing and spiritual saturation of the gospel in this world, that is, a millennial reign of Christ through his church here on earth. Postmillennialism has tended to be more popular during times of revival and prosperity in the Christian church.

Regardless of your interpretation of some of the specific aspects of the end times, we should all be able to agree that believers in Christ must remain fully assured that Jesus will come, and for those who have put their faith in him, it will be a glorious and joyful day. Thus, whatever we personally believe about the tribulation and the millennium, I hope we can all say together: the return of Christ demands constant, hopeful expectancy, and when he does come, Christians should not be found idle but busy at *his* work in *his* world in service to *him*.

(4) Reformed Theology

If we weren't already wading through controversial material, we certainly are about to as we talk about Reformed theology. But before we talk about this one, let me just reiterate that we are discussing these issues because we care. We think it will be helpful, both as you get to know our church and as you mature in your understanding of Christianity.

Reformed theology is a rose (or some might say a thorn) that goes by several names, such as "the doctrines of grace" or Calvinism (as opposed to Arminianism).

In the book *Bloodlines: Race, Cross, and the Christian*, author John Piper claims that he loves Reformed theology the way he might love a picture of his wife. The point Piper makes is that he does not love the picture of his wife in and of itself. He doesn't love ink on paper or pixels on a screen. Rather, he loves the picture because it is an accurate portrayal of the woman he does love. Similarly, when he says, "I love Reformed theology," Piper means that it reveals God in that "It's the best composite, Bible-distilled picture of God [he] has" (p. 130). In short, he doesn't love doctrines on paper but the God these doctrines describe.

But what is Reformed theology? What is this "Bible-distilled picture of God" that Piper is talking about?

As Piper answers the question in the subsequent pages, he focuses his explanation on what he calls "two defining clusters of beliefs" that make up what he considers to be at the core of Reformed theology. Allow me to explain these two "clusters" below.

First, there is a commitment to the five great solas that came out of the Reformation which took place in Europe during the 1500s (*sola* is Latin for "alone"). The five solas are:

Sola Scriptura, Scripture Alone
Solus Christus, Christ Alone
Sola Gratia, Grace Alone
Sola Fide, Faith Alone
Soli Deo Gloria, To the Glory of God Alone

Piper weaves the underlying meaning of these individual phrases into one unified meaning with the statement:

> God's justification of sinners is by *grace* alone, through *faith* alone, because of *Christ* alone, to the *glory of God* alone, on the authority of *Scripture* alone. (p. 131, emphasis original)

If you read the material on justification in Week 1, then you can probably already guess that we give a hearty "Amen!" to this statement.

The second "cluster of defining beliefs" that define Reformed theology is often called the five points of Calvinism. Frequently, these points are taught using the acronym T-U-L-I-P, which stands for total depravity, unconditional election, limited atonement, irresistible grace, and perseverance of the saints. Perhaps there are better ways to describe these doctrines, but TULIP is the one that seems to have stuck. In short, these five points place emphasis on God's sovereignty in salvation—from beginning to end. This is why the doctrines of grace are sometimes described as "Big God Theology."

Having a large view of God and his sovereignty, however, does not mean we believe human responsibility is unimportant. Human responsibility is very important. We are not robots. The Bible makes this very clear.

I would love to continue this discussion, but this simply isn't the place. Besides, if I gave this topic more space right now, it might imply something we certainly wouldn't want to imply. If we gave the next ten pages to this topic, it might give the impression to those who understand the relationship between God's sovereignty and human responsibility differently than our pastor-elders, as Arminians do, that we discourage them from attending our church or that we hope to exclude them from membership. That's absolutely not the case. On all of the issues listed in this section, we strongly desire that our church would be a community that appreciates and supports discussion, not shuts it down. And that's why we are discussing things now. Feel free to bring up questions about Reformed theology in class.

(5) Complementarianism

Making a distinction between men's and women's roles is especially controversial in our day. But this is nothing new. It's often been the case. We see this even in the New Testament itself. We shouldn't have a romantic view of the early church. They too needed to work through the issues, just as we do. Thankfully, God did not leave them to fend for themselves. God gave them his Word, just as he has given it to us.

There are two main theological positions on men's and women's roles in the Christian church. They go by the names of "complementarianism" and "egalitarianism." Let me start by saying what both of these views affirm. Both views affirm that men and women are created equally in the image of God and, consequently, have equal dignity, value, and worth. Both views believe that women and men can, and should, participate in significant ways in Christian ministry. The Danvers Statement, which is a complementarian statement of faith, says this clearly:

> With half the world's population outside the reach of indigenous evangelism; with countless other lost people in those societies that have heard the gospel; with the stresses and miseries of sickness, malnutrition, homelessness, illiteracy, ignorance, aging, addiction, crime, incarceration, neuroses, and loneliness, no *man* or *woman* who feels a passion from God to make His grace known in word and deed need ever live without a fulfilling ministry for the glory of Christ and the good of this fallen world (1 Corinthians 12:7–21). (Danvers Statement, Affirmation IX, 1987; emphasis added)

In short, both complementarians and egalitarians believe that God does give both men and women extraordinary gifts for ministry.

And yet, there *are* differences in the two positions. Egalitarians believe that there should be *no* distinctions in roles in the home and the church that are based on the innate qualities of gender, but rather that any and all roles should be decided on the basis of competency. In other words, if you are good at something, regardless of your gender, then you should be able to do it.

Complementarians don't believe this. They believe that manhood, in distinction from womanhood, means something—something beautiful. And complementarians believe that womanhood, in distinction from manhood, means something—something beautiful. But what are these distinctions? Space does not allow us to explore this in detail, but in principle, we believe that the Bible describes masculinity and femininity in this way:

> Masculinity: At the heart of mature masculinity is a sense of benevolent responsibility to lead, provide for, and protect women in ways appropriate to a man's differing relationships.

> Femininity: At the heart of mature femininity is a freeing disposition to affirm, receive, and nurture strength and leadership from worthy men in ways appropriate to a woman's differing relationships.

These definitions are taken from the definitive complementarian work on the topic entitled *Recovering Biblical Manhood & Womanhood* by John Piper and Wayne Grudem (Chapter 1: "A Vision of Biblical Complementarity").

At Community, one of the ways that complementarianism expresses itself is in the belief that God has left the office of elder open only to men.

Because this is such a controversial point for many, allow me to mention a few of the biblical reasons for this view. Biblical support for male eldership is seen in the following:

> the responsibilities given by God to Adam before and after the fall (Genesis 2–3; Romans 5:12ff.);

> the pattern of Old Testament and New Testament spiritual leadership being placed mainly among men;

> the parallels between male leadership in the church and the headship of men in the home as taught in places like Ephesians 5, Colossians 3, and Titus 2;

> no explicit mention of female pastor-elders in the New Testament;

> and, finally, specific passages like 1 Timothy 2:8–3:7 and Titus 1:5–9 which require male pastor-elders.

As with the topic of the millennium above, let me end the topic of men's and women's roles by underscoring what we all should believe: men and women are equal in dignity, value, and worth, and as such, should participate in significant Christian ministry in every church, including ours.

BACKING UP TO GO FORWARD

In seminary, my best friend was Bryan. When Bryan and I were first getting to know each other, he commented to me, "Oh yeah, you're in the E-Free Church. That's the denomination where you can believe anything you want, as long as you are premillennial."

I told him that wasn't exactly true.

Then he added, "But don't you have 'that Carson guy' in your denomination?" as though that made us a little more legit. "That Carson guy" is Dr. D. A. Carson, one of the best evangelical New Testament scholars in the world. So yes, since he is a leader in our denomination, perhaps it does make us more legit—at least to seminary students.

But if my seminary friend Bryan didn't know much about the EFCA, then you probably don't know much either. So let's talk briefly about the history of our denomination as well as our own church's history. And then we'll end by talking about where Community is headed in the future.

A brief history of the Evangelical Free Church of America

When studying historical movements, one has to choose a place to start. This is always difficult because one event influences another, and another, and so on. For example, to talk about the early church in the city of Ephesus, one could look at what John wrote in Revelation 2:1–7, or one could look earlier at 1 & 2 Timothy (Timothy was a pastor in Ephesus), or one could look at Paul's instructions to the Ephesian elders in Acts 20, or one could look earlier to Paul's letter to the Ephesians, or earlier still to Paul's conversion in Acts 9, or maybe even to Matthew 28, or … on and on until you're in Genesis!

So, where did the EFCA come from? Shall we start with the official merger in 1950? That would at least start us in America, and after all, we are the Evangelical Free Church of *America*. Or shall we begin across the Atlantic Ocean in Europe, or more specifically, two particular countries, namely, Sweden and Norway in the 1800s? Or shall we begin with the influence of the sixteenth-century Reformation?

Let's save the Reformation for another time and start in Sweden and Norway. In the 1800s there was growing dissatisfaction among many Christians in Sweden over the practices of the state church, specifically in regards to baptism and the Lord's Supper. At that time in Sweden, the birth of a child was not recognized by the state until the child was baptized in an official state church. In other words, instead of a birth certificate from a hospital, they had baptism certificates from government-sanctioned churches. This was a problem. And increasingly so because many of the clergy were known to be unconverted. Thus, many Christians were asking themselves questions like this: "Should Christians be force-fed the Bible and holy communion from unbelievers?"

It's hard for us as Americans to fully understand this integration of church and state, but groups that were precursors to the EFCA were forged at a time when, as Calvin Hanson writes, "attendance at communion was required by law" (*What It Means to Be Free!*, p. 37). Yet in the midst of this, the Swedish church experienced revival, a revival that continued as many sought religious freedom in America. Similar events were taking place in Norway and Denmark (both in state church dysfunction and "free" church revival).

As these European Christians came to the United States, they began to organize and form congregations. In the early 1900s, there were several attempts to merge two associations, the Swedish Evangelical Free Church and the Norwegian-Danish Evangelical Free Church. And in June of 1950, it was official: a merger happened, and the EFCA was born. At the time of the merger, the EFCA adopted a twelve-point statement of faith, which remained unchanged until 2008. On June 26, 2008, in St. Louis, Missouri, I and almost one thousand other EFCA delegates voted to adopt a new statement of faith. This statement of faith, while good, was not inclusive of the full breadth of orthodox positions on eschatology (the doctrine of last things). This inspired the EFCA to, on June 19, 2019, approve our current statement of faith (the one used earlier in this chapter).

Today the term "free" carries a slightly different nuance in the EFCA than it did in Sweden, but the spirit of freedom continues in the way a local congregation rules its own body. Free from denominational constraints, each congregation decides on theological matters deemed to be of second- and third-order importance. At Community, this means our membership must vote on things such as amending the constitution and bylaws, calling and affirming pastor-elders, approving the budget, and buying and selling property. You can read more about the specifics in the appendix, "Bylaws of the Community Evangelical Free Church." And speaking of Community, let's talk for a moment about our history.

A brief history of Community Evangelical Free Church

On September 12, 1999, about 75 believers met for Community's first public worship service. It was held in the gym of Northside Elementary School on Devonshire Road in Colonial Park.

But much planning, prayer, and hard work were put in long before that first service was realized. The church plant was the culmination of two years of preparation by Hershey Evangelical Free Church, work led by associate pastor Kevin Dixon and his wife Lori. They had felt the Lord leading them to plant a church somewhere in the Colonial Park area that would be actively evangelistic, equip saints for ministry, and foster a caring, one-another atmosphere. After much prayer, Pastor Kevin shared his vision with the Hershey Free Church elder board, and they enthusiastically gave their blessing.

Over the years, God has been so very faithful to our little church. He's grown our congregation from a nomadic church plant into a fixture of the Lawnton community, and now one in

Susquehanna Township; he's provided many gifted leaders to teach and disciple and grow us; and he's continuing to increase our faith in Jesus and grow our service to Jesus, whether in Harrisburg or around the world.

Going Forward: Multiplying churches

As we say on our website, we are not perfect; we are not flashy; we are not the best or the brightest of people. Our story is obviously in progress, but that doesn't mean that we don't know its ultimate goal or end. We do. As Christians, we believe that our story is tied to the Big Story—the story of the good news of God's love for sinners, a story centered on the person and work of Jesus. That story has a happy ending.

Therefore, in this in-between time, the time before the return of Jesus, we will continue to strive to be an authentic community of Christ followers who welcome the fellowship of other Christians and attempt to answer honestly the questions of sincerely interested non-Christians.

To accomplish this, we would love nothing more than to be a church that plants other churches—churches that, in turn, also plant other churches. In fact, it's always been this way in Christianity. In the early church through the beginnings of the EFCA, churches planting churches that plant other churches is a chief way in which God's love expands in this world. And we want to do our part in this; we want to plant churches that plant other churches.

We'd love for you to help us.

I will build my church, and the gates of hell shall not prevail against it.

- Jesus

THE IMPORTANCE OF BEING CONNECTED

I lived in St. Louis for several years, and even more so than in Harrisburg, the highways were surrounded with billboards. Most billboards displayed the types of advertising we are accustomed to, but not all. Some were different. Some of the billboards were maintained by the Missouri Department of Transportation, or MoDOT (Missouri's counterpart to PennDOT).

These billboards stood out because they didn't have glossy pictures and catchy sayings. Instead, they looked like big digital watches—black backgrounds with large orange text. Normally MoDOT billboards simply give traffic information:

13 MIN TO INTERSTATE 270 VIA INTERSTATE 170

22 MIN TO AIRPORT

LANE CLOSURE AT HIGHWAY 40 & GRAND

However, on rare occasions, they tragically read:

MISSING CHILD ALERT

I'm confident that a missing child alert, an "AMBER Alert" as they are called now, is a big deal everywhere, but it's especially so in St. Louis. In the decade while I lived in St. Louis, the city had several highly publicized incidents involving missing children (Shawn Hornbeck, for example, who was rescued in 2007 after four years of captivity).

Sometimes, as I was driving home from work to be with my family, I would see those bright orange letters (MISSING CHILD ALERT) and my thoughts would drive away from me. I'd think to myself,

> Right now, as I drive home to be with my family, there is another home where a dad is driving home to be with his family, but a little boy or a little girl is *missing.*

> A child who is part of a family—a child who has a unique fingerprint, and hair and eye color, and brothers and sisters—is missing.

> A boy who plays with baseballs and G.I. Joes or a girl who plays with dolls and jewelry is *MISSING.* And right now parents are grieving and scared and confused because a child, who is part of their family, *is not home for dinner!*

But then, nearly lost in my thoughts, I'd snap back to reality as a car in front of me would tap its breaks. *Oh yeah, I'm in rush hour traffic. Pay attention, Benjamin, pay attention.*

THE CHURCH AS FAMILY AND BODY

In reflecting on the tragedy of a missing child, certain parallels can be seen with the tragedy that occurs all too often in Christianity. The tragedy is this: a family member is missing.

Let me explain. The Bible teaches that to be a Christian does not simply mean that you become connected to God through faith. It means this, but it also means more. To be a Christian means being connected to other Christians. Different metaphors are used in the Bible to depict this reality, but two prominent ones are *family* and *body*.

Using the family metaphor, the Bible teaches that to be a Christian means that one has become part of the family of which all other Christians are a part because all Christians have God as their Father. Using the body metaphor, the Bible teaches that to be a Christian means that you are part of the same body—as a hand, foot, and elbow are all connected to the same body. This is true, the Bible teaches, because Jesus "is the head of the body, the church" (Colossians 1:18).

In other words, the Bible teaches that to be a Christian *is* to be a part of the family of God and a part of the body of Christ. Christians do not have to try to become a family or a body; by virtue of their connection to God through faith in Christ, they just are.

Now here is where the tragedy occurs. When a Christian, who is positionally part of the family of God, is not connected in practical ways to this family, we might say that they are "missing," that there's an AMBER Alert and that a tragedy is taking place.

And we might say that when a person has been attached to the body of Christ through faith, yet practically he or she has no contact with the body, this is like a disability for the whole church.

Thus, practical connection to the body of Christ is not a peripheral thing. Connection is not marginal. It matters. Lack of connection is a tragedy in desperate need of immediate remedy.

There are two very important implications to these realities that are worth stressing. First, just like appendages of a body, not every Christian has the same function. We all have different gifts and callings and thus not every Christian is called to participate and serve the body in the same way. This truth can be seen in Romans 12:4–5 where Paul writes,

> For as in one body we have many members, and the members do not all have the same function, so we, though many, are one body in Christ, and individually members one of another.

Similarly, in 1 Corinthians 12:17 Paul asks the rhetorical questions,

> If the whole body were an eye, where would be the sense of hearing? If the whole body were an ear, where would be the sense of smell?

These verses, and others like them, clearly show that every Christian has unique gifts. This should be a freeing reality. It means that you don't have to duplicate someone else's role in the church nor should we value one person's role over another. Every person matters.

Second, not only do different members have different functions but also—and this is obvious from the body metaphor—we are all connected. That is, when one part of the body hurts, so does the rest of the body.

If my right arm gets a cut and begins to bleed severely, then my left arm does not look at my right arm and say, "That's your problem!" This does not happen because, needless to say, the well-being of one arm is united to the well-being of the other.

Conversely, if in another circumstance my left arm is broken, and my right arm is not, then the strong arm can pick up food and drink off the table and put it in my mouth so that both arms benefit, not simply the strong arm.

Thus, the overall health of one particular member of Community really matters to every other member of Community. If one Christian is hurting or living in sin, it really matters to the rest of us because we are part of the same family and body. You cannot have sickness or sin in one appendage without affecting the whole body! But on the other hand, when one member is healthy and serving the Lord, everyone at Community benefits. As Paul says, "If one member suffers, all suffer together; if one member is honored, all rejoice together" (1 Corinthians 12:26).

HOW TO SHARE GOD-CENTERED TESTIMONIES

At this point, let's transition to the final topic of the class, namely, how to share what God has done in your life. I mentioned this at the start of the book. Perhaps some of you have been dreading it ever since then because you know this means that you'll be asked to talk in front of others, especially about personal things.

As I said then, I hope you don't feel that way. But if you do, please know that we want to prepare you for this as best we can. I have offered coaching to people about this in the past, and it seems to make a huge difference. In fact, when I've had people share their stories in a God-centered way, whether in a membership class or a small group Bible study setting, it tends to be everyone's favorite part. But before I give some specific coaching, we need to back up just a bit to see our individual stories in the context of the Big Story of the Bible, the story of the mission of God.

The Mission of God

There's an old hymn that speaks of Christian soldiers "marching on." That's good. We can and should march on. But Christians must recognize that we "march on" only because God marches on. God is the one on a mission, first and foremost.

Sometimes God's mission is more overt and sometimes more covert, but his mission advances and his kingdom spreads. Though it starts as small as a mustard seed, it grows … and it grows … and it grows. In the end, as Jesus said, the little seed becomes "larger than all the garden plants and becomes a tree" (Matthew 13:32). And what a strong tree it becomes, one where "the birds of the air come and make nests in its branches." This verse, and others like it, reminds us that one day the prayer Jesus taught us to pray will be answered and God's kingdom will come in its fullness and his desires will be carried out on earth as they are in heaven (Matthew 6:5ff.).

We see then that God is on a mission—the mission to redeem his creation and to vindicate the honor of his name. What was lost with the fall of Adam and Eve in the garden is won back in the gospel of Jesus Christ. And for this, we are thankful.

Just think for a moment what our world would be like if this were not so, if God were not on a mission to redeem. Think what it would be like if God were aloof and anemic. It is not a pretty picture. But fortunately, God did not let Adam and Eve drift away after their sin. He went after them. He looked for them. "Adam, where are you?" God asked (Genesis 3:9).

God didn't have to look. God didn't have to search for a rebellious sinner like Adam. God simply could have let him go. But God went on a mission.

Today, the mission of God continues. Yes, all is not as it should be, but one day it will be, and "the earth will be filled with the knowledge of the glory of the Lord as the waters cover the sea" (Habakkuk 2:14).

And for the promise of that day—and every bit of progress toward it—we are thankful.

Sharing God-Centered Testimonies

Every Christian has a special place in the story of God's redemptive mission. In fact, this is part of what it means to be a Christian, namely, someone who has experienced firsthand the mission of God to redeem.

In Psalm 107:2 the author pleads with the people of God to make their part in God's mission, as recipients of his grace, known to others. The verse reads: "Let the redeemed of the Lord say so!" As the psalm continues, we read of different groups of people that God has redeemed. And then in the final verse of the psalm, we read this command: "Whoever is wise, let him attend to these things, let them consider the steadfast love of the LORD" (v. 43). In the context, the phrase "these things" must mean that those who are wise will listen closely to the stories of how God has redeemed his people. In other words, listening to testimonies of how God has saved people is a vital part of our life together. It's one avenue whereby we "consider the steadfast love of the LORD."

Many people feel intimidated when they think of sharing how God has worked in their lives. One reason for this is because extraordinary stories of people with sordid pasts tend to grab our attention in such a way that we often view our own journey to faith as comparatively tame and even boring.

Sometimes I've joked that a "good testimony" needs to sound like this:

> Once upon a time, I lived a life of sin and rebellion as a drug lord in a cartel. I lived fast and loose: women, money, and pleasure. After years of this life, when I was eighteen years old, my arm was blown off during a confrontation with a rival gang.

> But then I came to Jesus and, lo' and behold, my arm actually grew back! Jesus is amazing! Now, at the age of twenty, I am a changed man.

Of course the above anecdote is meant to be humorous, but it does reflect, albeit with thick sarcasm, what Christians often think makes a great testimony.

But I can assure you that there is no such thing as a tame story of God's saving work, even for those that grow up in a Christian home. When the mission of God to redeem a broken sinner by washing them in waves of hope and forgiveness occurs, nothing is boring about it. Nothing.

What I have found is that with a little examination and reflection, even those of us who have previously considered our story bland can come to see the hand of God upon our lives in exciting and significant ways. And that's what I want to help you do in this final section; I want to help you begin to craft a gospel-centered version of the story of how God has been, and continues to be, at work in your life. Many of you will have done something like this before, but perhaps doing it again will remind you afresh of how God's mission to redeem has transformed your life.

First, try to think of ten significant moments in your life. If you can't think of ten, think of eight or perhaps just five. There is no special significance to the number ten. The important thing is to concretely identify a number of events in your life that have shaped who you are today and continue to shape who you'll be in the future.

Each of these moments or seasons in your life may be significant in different ways and for different reasons. Perhaps one person will recall a time where they experienced tremendous growth, while another significant moment may involve a major setback. A significant moment for you may have been moving away for college or the loss of a dear friend due to illness. Possibly it's when your parents got divorced or when you were divorced. Perhaps times of great joy come to mind and, again, perhaps times of great sorrow.

Here is another way to think about how to identify these moments. Picture your life as a continuous movie reel. When you do this, ask what moments in the movie you would want to slow down—perhaps even hit the "pause button"—so that more explanation could be given to any one particular scene. Those are likely key moments for you.

With these thoughts in mind, please take time to reflect on your life and list as many significant moments as you can below.

1. _____

2. _____

3. _____

4. _____

5. _____

6. _____

7. _____

8. _____

9. _____

10. _____

If you are like most people, the list you just created is full of memories that are very precious (or maybe painful) to you.

The next step in crafting a gospel-centered retelling of your story of God's grace is to begin reflecting on where and how God was working in each of these moments or events. Take the time to move through the list, asking of each event this question: "What was God doing in this event or season?"

It is not an easy question to answer. It will likely take some time. And even after giving the necessary time to reflect upon it, I should note that we'll never know the answer to this question exhaustively. In fact, there are significant moments in my life where I feel like the "jury is still out," and I am not fully aware of *all* that God was doing or even *some* of what God was doing. This is likely true of you as well.

However, I suspect that when you look at the items placed on the list, you will be able to identify some special ways that God was working—perhaps overtly and perhaps covertly—through these moments in your life.

We sometimes say around our church that everyone has a two-minute version of their story and a two-hour version, and everything in between. As you consider how to tell your story in the fourth week of class (and in the membership interview with the pastor-elders), we're looking for the five-minute version. To get to this place, you're going to have to leave a lot out. So, just pick three or so of these moments to share, noting that even with just picking three, there still will not be time to explain every detail.

Also, as you linger on one of the moments, try to include within the telling of your story some of the elements of the gospel and how Christians come into a relationship with God. So many times when I hear people tell their story, they give the impression that their story and their salvation is really about them. But that's not true. People are saved by trusting what God has done on their behalf in the death and resurrection of Jesus. We want to make sure that's the story we are telling. If you need to, you might find it helpful to review the gospel as discussed extensively in Week 1. It's not necessary, however, that you include the same words or phrases that I used. Rather, try to distill the concepts into your own words, words that are familiar to you and part of your natural vocabulary. This will give your story a natural feel.

Additionally, while I readily acknowledge that the thought of physically writing your story out will not excite everyone, I do know that for some it may be a helpful, even necessary, exercise.

Finally, as we close this last section, I want to stress something vital: We have not encouraged sharing your story of God's grace simply because we need one more prerequisite in our membership process. We do not.

On the contrary, if you are a Christian, the grace of God has worked in your life in powerful ways, and we believe taking the time to develop your ability to tell this story well is a worthwhile endeavor for many reasons.

First, it will encourage your own heart as you see the way God is working in your life. Second, it has the potential to encourage those around you in your daily life, even some who are not yet Christians. Finally, God delights in the telling of God-centered testimonies because they give him the honor and glory that he rightly deserves. The Bible itself has whole chapters devoted to retelling significant moments of redemption in the lives of the people of God, either corporately or individually (e.g., Psalm 106 and Acts 26:12ff.).

Below is an example of how I often share my story. It's just shy of 300 words, so it's about the three-minute version. I offer it to you not as the perfect model of how to tell a God-centered testimony but simply as an attempt to be helpful, an attempt to give a demonstration of using significant moments in your life to clarify how the mission of God to redeem has washed over you.

As you read it, notice that I added numbers in brackets to indicate a few of the significant moments that I put on my "top ten" list. Also, in the section where I stress the gospel, I added a [G].

I grew up in a Christian family [1], but I only embraced the externals of the faith, that is, until my junior year of college. Just prior to that time, everything started to come unraveled at the seams [2]. My world—which revolved around academics, athletics, and a relationship with a girlfriend—fell apart. All three were letting me down, and it hurt. Bad.

In the spring of my junior year, by God's grace, I began to attend a Bible study in the athletic department [3]. After the semester, I attended a Christian sports camp in Colorado [4]. There I was surrounded by people who actually cared about all the things I knew I was supposed to care about but never did. They also seemed to have a deep joy, which I certainly did not. I left the camp with a determination to follow Christ; I ended my relationship with my longtime girlfriend and began to read the Bible for the first time as an adult [5].

In those next few months, I saw my sin as offensive not just to man, but to God. I saw Jesus as the Savior whose death and resurrection was real and sufficient for my sins. Through repentance and faith, eternal life was offered, which I gladly received [G].

Over the next few years, God nudged me slowly, but assuredly, into ministry; I led *this* and spoke at *that*. Ten years ago, an EFCA pastor helped me to preach my first sermon [7]. I have sensed my call to ministry through my own passion and gifting in ministry, which others around me have confirmed.

It has been a blessing to use and refine these gifts during my time at Covenant Theological Seminary in St. Louis, MO [8a] and pastoral ministry at Salem EFCA in St.

Louis, MO [8b], New Life Bible Fellowship in Tucson, AZ [9], and here at Community [10].

Perhaps as we teach this class in years to come, we may be able to collect several examples of how others share their gospel-story. If that is something you are willing to do, please let me know.

For now, I hope you enjoy listening to others around your table as you learn of the continuance of God's mission to redeem. May your hearts be strengthened by stories of personal redemption as the "redeemed of the Lord say so."

HOW TO LEAVE A CHURCH WELL

We've just spent three weeks talking about what it means to join a church generally and specifically to join our church. We've talked about what we believe about all sorts of theological doctrines, from the gospel to the EFCA statement of faith, and we even touched on premillennialism, Reformed theology, and complementarianism. We've talked about where our denomination has been, how our church was planted, and how, in the future, we'd also like to plant churches. We've talked about the importance of being practically connected to God's body, the local church, and we have talked about the story God has given you to share. As I said at the start, this was our attempt to love you well. You need to know what you are getting into when you join a church. It's not a small decision.

But we're not done yet; there is one more thing to cover.

We live in transient times. People can so quickly change cell phone numbers, email addresses, and even houses, jobs, and careers. In today's culture, there are simply not many things that have permanence, even from a human perspective, and this includes loyalty to a local church.

All of this is not necessarily a bad thing, but it does create the need for a conversation about how to leave a church well. In this short epilogue, our purpose is not to delve into all the potential reasons for leaving a church—the good, the bad, and the ugly. But given the fact that, unless you and I die while at Community, at some point in our lives we will all likely move on to another church for one reason or another.

We ask that when the time does arrive, you make the necessary effort to leave Community well. What "well" looks like will vary from situation to situation. Perhaps it involves a simple phone call to the church office to let us know. Or perhaps it involves a longer conversation with members of the pastoral staff.

Because we really do care about you, we don't simply want you to fade away or, worse yet, to leave with feelings of resentment, hurt, or unresolved conflict. Leaving a church poorly is not good for anybody—the person, the particular church from which you leave, and even the next church that you join. In fact, if you didn't leave well from your previous church, it's not too late. God wants you to do so because when we talk about the church, we're talking about Jesus's bride.

And as God loves you, we love you. So, if you should decide to become connected to our fellowship, great. But please love us enough in return to leave well, if and when the time comes.

CONSTITUTION

ARTICLE I: NAME

The name of this church will be Community Evangelical Free Church of Harrisburg, Pennsylvania.

ARTICLE II: STATEMENT OF FAITH

Adopted by the Conference on June 19, 2019. [Note the EFCA Statement of Faith has not been reprinted here because it appears in Week 2.]

ARTICLE III: PURPOSE

The purpose of Community Evangelical Free Church of Harrisburg is to develop fully devoted followers of Jesus Christ by: winning people to faith in Jesus Christ, connecting believers in Christian community, building members in their faith in Jesus Christ, and sending maturing followers out into the world to labor for Jesus Christ.

ARTICLE IV: AFFILIATION

The congregation is affiliated with the "Evangelical Free Church of America, Incorporated" for the purpose of pursuing mutual objectives with the said Evangelical Free Church of America.

ARTICLE V: MEMBERSHIP

This church shall receive as members those who have accepted Jesus Christ as their personal Lord and Savior, being born again, and who in their lives are manifesting the fruits of a true faith in God. They must also be willing to uphold the responsibilities of membership and affirm the statement of faith as stated in our constitution.

ARTICLE VI: OFFICERS

The pastor-elders and deacons/deaconesses will be responsible for guiding the affairs of the church. The pastor-elders and deacons/deaconesses who govern the Community Evangelical Free Church of Harrisburg will consist of church members who are affirmed by the congregation for appointment as pastor-elders and deacons/deaconesses. The officers will consist of a Chairman and Secretary from the pastor-elders and a Treasurer from the Deacon-Deaconess Board.

ARTICLE VII: CHURCH GOVERNMENT

All authority in the church is vested in the voting membership of the church, hereafter referred to in this constitution and associated Bylaws as the congregation. The congregation shall decide upon the call of the pastor-elders, the purchase or sale of church real property, the selection of deacons, the establishment of fiscal budgets, and other such matters as it shall determine. There will be an annual meeting of the congregation to be conducted one month prior to the beginning of the church's fiscal year for the purpose of affirming pastor-elders and other leaders and establishing a budget. The Chairman can call other congregational meetings with a two-week prior notice to the congregation. Quorum requirements will be stated in the bylaws.

ARTICLE VIII: PROPERTY RIGHTS

The church shall have the power to buy, sell, own, receive by gift or purchase, hold and dispose of or encumber any and all personal or real property as authorized by the bylaws and under the State of Pennsylvania, as deemed necessary by the church board for business purposes and with permission of the church. All such property shall be held in the name of the church.

ARTICLE IX: DISSOLUTION

In the event that the members vote to dissolve the church corporation, all right, title, and interest in the property and other assets of the said congregation will be transferred to the Eastern District Association of the Evangelical Free Church of America, providing that the said association is in agreement with the provisions of this constitution. This will transpire after all fiscal responsibility is provided for any employees and/or missionaries of the church. The Chairman, Vice-Chairman, Secretary, and Treasurer holding office at the time such dissolution is voted will be authorized to act with full powers on behalf of said church corporation in making such transfer of property and assets effective.

ARTICLE X: AMENDMENTS

Amendments to this constitution may be made at any regularly scheduled meeting of the congregation by a four-fifths (4/5) majority of votes cast, provided said proposed amendments have been presented in writing and discussed at a meeting of the congregation at least one month prior to the time when the vote on the changes is taken.

BYLAWS

A PASSION FOR THE WORD OF GOD

The Bible is our foundation and source of inspired and inerrant truth. We want to be known as a people with an unquenchable thirst for knowing and loving God more deeply (Philippians 3:8). Following Jesus is no mere intellectual pursuit, but one born out of astonishment at the grace of God as it is expressed in the gospel and revealed in our fellowship. Because all of theology is practical, the adherence to sound doctrine and the application of biblical truth is an ultimately useful endeavor.

GOSPEL-CENTEREDNESS

The gospel is the good news that Jesus Christ lived the life we should have lived, died the death we should have died, and rose again defeating death forever (1 Corinthians 15:3–4). By grace alone, through faith alone, and in Christ alone, we receive the gift of salvation. When our record of sin was taken by Christ to the cross, Jesus received the wrath of God and rejection that we deserved and, in turn, his perfect life and record is transferred to our account. (2 Corinthians 5:21). Astonishment at this amazing grace should be the heartbeat of every ministry of the church—informing and shaping the way we go about even the smallest details of ministry (1 Corinthians 15:1–2).

AUTHENTIC COMMUNITY

A community that believes the gospel should be one marked by the grace of God and one that consists of deep, authentic, and caring relationships. Because we're saved by grace alone (not by anything we've done), we're freed to admit who we really are—the worst of sinners (1 Timothy 1:15) —and, therefore, enabled to embody a culture of repentance, forgiveness, growth in Christlikeness, prayer, and joy (Acts 2:46–47).

MISSIONAL LIVING

Everyone who comes to trust in Christ is a minister of the gospel (2 Corinthians 5:18). Every facet of life should be viewed as an opportunity to display the all-surpassing worth of Jesus Christ, and no area of our lives—work, play, church events, or small group fellowships—should be separated from our mission to make disciples and spread the good news. Our community does not exist simply to create deep relationships within our own congregation but to be directed outward in mission. This mission to see disciples multiplied has also given us a desire to be a church that eventually plants other gospel-centered churches in Harrisburg and its surrounding areas.

HUMBLE-SERVICE

Though we enthusiastically desire that all would know Christ, we are called to love and serve others in our city regardless of whether they follow Jesus or not. Christ's love for outsiders, like us (Romans 5:8), must urge our fellowship toward acts of service, care for the poor, and a willingness to lay our lives down for our neighbors.

ARTICLE I: MEMBERSHIP

1. MEMBERSHIP PROCEDURE

1. Prospective members commit to attend the membership classes taught by the pastor-elders.
2. Application for membership is made to the pastor-elders.
3. The pastor-elders arrange a meeting with the applicant(s), who give an oral testimony of conversion and personal faith. The pastor-elders have the option of discussing with the applicant(s) whether their Christian experience and doctrinal beliefs are consistent with the scriptural principles found in our statement of faith (Article II, Constitution).
4. The list of applicants for membership is presented to the congregation at least two weeks prior to acceptance so that any member in good standing may notify the pastor-elders in the event of a substantiated objection.
5. Should a church member object to an applicant for membership, the member will state the reason to the pastor-elders. The pastor-elders will discuss any objections at a confidential meeting. If it is determined that any objections warrant further discussion the matter will be handled with sensitivity, confidentiality, and love. The pastor-elders will appoint a pastor-elder to specifically handle each membership issue.

6. Having allowed for congregational response, the pastor-elders have the authority to accept for membership the applicants they consider qualified on the basis of their testimony of conversion, confession of faith, and demonstrated lifestyle.

7. The accepted applicant(s) are publicly received into membership and charged with the duties of membership at one of the public worship services.

2. RESPONSIBILITIES AND DUTIES OF MEMBERSHIP

With the privilege of membership come certain duties and responsibilities. We at CEFCH expect that our members will be characterized by the following:

1. Participation in Christian community (e.g., small group, other ministry groups, etc.)

2. Attendance at church worship services and congregational meetings.

3. Development and use of their gifts from the Holy Spirit to minister to others.

4. Prayer for other members, pastor-elders, leaders of the church, and the lost.

5. Generous financial support of the work of the church as God has given generously to us.

6. A life marked by an abiding and active love for Jesus.

7. A growing knowledge of the Word while bearing witness in the world.

8. Loving one another, demonstrating a servant's heart, and following the loving authority of our church leaders.

3. CHURCH RESPONSIBILITY TO MEMBERS

As God enables, the church will provide:

1. Sound biblical teaching.
2. Regular and varied opportunities for corporate worship.
3. A small group in which members can be cared for and grow.
4. A welcoming, warm, and respectful place to bring family, friends, co-workers, and acquaintances.
5. Opportunity to be equipped/trained for ministry.
6. The means for discovery of spiritual gifts and opportunities in which to utilize each believer's gifts.
7. If requested by a member, a letter of recommendation from a pastor-elder, on behalf of the pastor-elders as a whole, will be given to any member who leaves the church in good standing.

4. DISCIPLINE AND REMOVAL OF MEMBERSHIP

Should a pastor-elder or any member bring dishonor upon or be an offense to the church, by way of a sinful and ungodly life or by heresy, his or her membership may be terminated if the pastor-elders so decide. The church membership shall be notified of the decision of the pastor-elders. However, the person in question will first be counseled and disciplined in a loving and Christian spirit according to Matthew 18:15–18; Galatians 6:1,2; Titus 3:10,11; and 1 Timothy 5:19–22, so that he or she may be restored to the will of God. In the case of a staff member who has come under discipline and, therefore, needs to stepdown from his or her position, the pastor-elders can determine to compensate the staff member, as a show of God's grace, for up to three months during his or her transition from ministry.

A member whose membership was terminated because of a sinful life may reapply for membership if the elders determine there is evidence that he or she has become repentant and is living in fellowship with God.

Members who absent themselves from Christian community and who fail to support or participate in the congregation's program (life of the church) may be removed from membership after the pastor-elders have attempted to resolve any problems or issues.

ARTICLE II: Pastor-Elders and Deacons & Deaconesses

1. PASTOR-ELDERS

A. The Office of Pastor-Elder

In accord with the New Testament, pastor-elders will oversee the spiritual welfare of the church. The number of pastor-elders will be determined by the number of men who are willing to serve and who are biblically qualified. Pastor-elders will be both paid and unpaid, determined by the need for full time staff to best shepherd the church. The pastor-elders will lead as a plurality with each sharing the same amount of authority. Availability and spiritual gifting will determine the amount of responsibility each man will be given. Each pastor-elder will be called by God and affirmed by the congregation. Each year, the congregation will reaffirm each current pastor-elder through a dedication service and affirm any new pastor-elder(s).

B. The Responsibilities of Pastor-Elders

The pastor-elders will be responsible for the spiritual nurture of the congregation. They will individually participate in particular ministries within the church and collectively guide the spiritual life of the church. They will be responsible for fostering spiritual growth and the pursuit of holiness by the members of the congregation, and they will form a unified team to pray and lead the church by example as a plurality of elders. Decisions, whenever possible, will be made by the consensus of pastor-elders in the spirit of humility and mutual submission. Pastor-elders will:

1. Shepherd the congregation as a team.
2. Devote their time to the equipping of the saints, teaching the Bible, and praying.
3. Oversee the public worship of the church and any activities of any group meeting in the name of the church or on the premises of the church.
4. Visit the sick and needy within the congregation and provide biblical counsel where needed.
5. Handle all matters of discipline as described in Article I.
6. Be responsible for commending to the congregation the call of pastor-elders.
7. Recommend biblically qualified deacons and deaconesses for affirmation by the congregation to fulfill their respective ministries (see Article II or III).
8. Be responsible for the activities of all ministry teams organized to oversee specific areas of ministries within the church.
9. The pastor-elder chairman will be the chief officer of the church. The chairman and secretary will be appointed by a majority vote of the pastor-elders.
10. Approve candidates for membership and be responsible for all additions to or deletions from the membership roll.
11. Affirm the yearly budget developed in conjunction with deacons before presenting to the congregation.
12. Non-staff pastor-elders will conduct an annual review of staff pastor-elders and their compensation, including things such as vacation and sabbatical policy.

C.   Nomination and Affirmation Process of Pastor-Elders

1.   Pastor-elders will be recommended on the basis of their general qualifications as a shepherd and their desire and ability to lead, instruct, and care for the flock in the fullness of the Holy Spirit. They must be members of the church, be in accord with the church's statement of faith and philosophy of ministry, and participate in a small group or similar ministry. As in the New Testament, they are to be men of exemplary Christian character and practice. Theirs will be a ministry of leadership based on their service to Christ and his Church. Their qualifications are described in 1 Timothy 3:1–7 and Titus 1:4–9.

2.   A member of the congregation may recommend another member as a proposed candidate by putting the recommendation in writing to the pastor-elders.

3.   Members who have been recommended for leadership will indicate their willingness to serve in writing to the pastor-elders.

4.   The pastor-elders will invite the recommended leaders to go through a training process to become a pastor-elder.

5.   The pastor-elders will discuss the qualifications, interview the recommended leaders, and choose by consensus those who meet the qualifications. The interview process will consist of issues of character and doctrine.

6.   After the training process and the interview, these recommended leaders will be presented to the congregation for affirmation at a congregational

meeting. The congregation will be notified five weeks in advance.

7. During the next three weeks, any member of the congregation will have opportunity to object to a recommended leader by letter to the pastor-elders.

8. A list of fully approved candidates (any objections to candidates having been reviewed by the pastor-elders) will be presented at the congregational meeting for a vote of affirmation on each candidate. An 80% affirmation will be required for a candidate to take office.

9. Pastor-elders will be affirmed annually with no term limit.

2. DEACON & DEACONESS

A. The Office of Deacon & Deaconess

The deacons and deaconesses will be recommended by the pastor-elders and affirmed by the congregation. They shall be responsible, under the authority of the pastor-elders, for the church properties and their maintenance. In addition they shall oversee the benevolent/caring ministries of the church body. They shall report as needed to the pastor-elders. Neither they nor the pastor-elders shall be empowered to deed, mortgage, buy, or sell a real property without authorization of the congregation. They will also be responsible to help develop the annual budget at the direction of the pastor-elders. There will be both a Secretary and a Treasurer of the Deacon Board, with the Treasurer coming from the Finance Team (see Article III).

B. The Responsibilities of Deacons & Deaconesses

1. Maintain and administer a benevolence fund to see that the material needs of the congregation (and others as

seen fit) are met according to our responsibilities as fellow believers and according to the guidelines established by the pastor-elders.

2. Supervise the caring ministries of the congregation. These responsibilities include ministering to the practical, physical needs of widows, single parents, homebound, elderly, and others as needs exist.

3. Keep all properties (including land, buildings, equipment, vehicles, etc.) in good repair, being empowered to spend up to $2,000 or up to $10,000 with pastor-elder approval. Expenditures beyond $10,000 must be submitted to the congregation for approval.

4. Manage the financial decisions of the church with pastor-elder input.

5. Make arrangements for food and lodging for visiting speakers and groups, funerals, and weddings (as requested). Make arrangements for meals to be delivered to needy members of our congregation following hospitalizations, during illness, etc.

6. Assist the pastor-elders in hospital visitations and home visitations to those who are ill, giving consideration to appropriateness of gender.

C. Nomination and Affirmation Process of Deacons & Deaconesses

1. Deacons and deaconesses will be recommended on the basis of their spiritual qualifications for leadership as stated in Acts 6:3, 1Timothy 3, and Titus. They must be members of the church, be in accord with the church's statement of faith and philosophy of ministry, and participate in a small group or similar ministry.

2. In addition to those candidates the pastor-elders seek out directly for the office, a member of the congregation may recommend another member as a proposed candidate by putting the recommendation in writing to the pastor-elders.

3. The pastor-elders will discuss the qualifications, interview a candidate, and choose by consensus those who meet the qualifications. The interview process will consist of issues of character and doctrine.

4. After a vetting process, recommended leaders will be presented to the congregation. The congregation will be notified five weeks in advance.

5. During the next three weeks, any member of the congregation will have opportunity to object to a recommended leader by letter to the pastor-elders.

6. A list of fully approved candidates (any objections to candidates having been reviewed by the pastor-elders) will be presented at the congregational meeting. Candidates will be affirmed annually by the pastor-elders with no term limit, though it is understood that there can be a sabbatical as the need arises.

ARTICLE III: MINISTRY TEAMS

A. This church regards as an integral part of itself all ministry teams and organizations which are formed from within the church and which use the church facilities.

B. Items of business from the ministry teams to be discussed at the pastor-elder meeting should be referred to the pastor-elders at least seven days prior to the regularly scheduled monthly pastor-elder meeting or be contained in a regular monthly report.

C. The pastor-elders must approve members of all standing ministry teams.

D. Additional ministry teams may be created as deemed necessary by the pastor-elders.

E. Standing Ministry Teams:

OUTREACH—responsible to develop, implement, and oversee the outreach program including the budget for outreach. Outreach ministry team members include men and women approved by the pastor-elders.

FINANCE—responsible to supervise the financial affairs of the church including presentation of an annual budget to the pastor/elders who, after accepting it, will present it for congregational approval. (Chaired by a deacon or deaconess serving as Treasurer; team members include men and women approved by the pastor-elders.)

ARTICLE IV: MEETINGS

A. Public church services shall be held at least once during the week.

B. Communion services shall be held at a minimum every other month at times established by the pastor-elders. Additional communion services shall be conducted at the discretion of the pastor-elders.

C. Pastor-elders shall meet monthly or more, as it deems necessary, and a majority of pastor-elders, constituting a quorum, shall be necessary to conduct a meeting.

D. Congregational business meetings shall be held once in the fall and as often as the need arises. Voting shall be limited to members of the congregation 18 years and older.

1. A quorum will consist of fifteen percent of the active, local membership.
2. Special congregational meetings may be called when either twenty-five members so request and sign a written notice or a majority of the pastor-elders issue a call. The notice of such meeting shall be posted for at least 14 days before any meeting.
3. All congregational meetings shall be conducted generally according to the biblical standards stated in Philippians chapter 2.

ARTICLE V: AMENDMENTS

Amendments to these bylaws can only be made at a regularly scheduled congregational meeting. The proposed bylaw must have been properly presented at a previous congregational meeting and recorded in the minutes thereof at least 28 days before the vote to adopt. A three-fourths (3/4) majority of votes cast is necessary to amend any bylaw.

Made in United States
North Haven, CT
27 October 2023

43263715R00052